STUDY GUIDE

Discover EPHESIANS

by
Deb Fennema

FAITH
ALIVE®
Christian Resources

Grand Rapids, Michigan

*I pray that out of his glorious riches [God the Father]
may strengthen you with power through his Spirit
in your inner being, so that Christ may dwell
in your hearts through faith.*

Ephesians 3:16-17

ISBN 1-56212-190-1

10 9 8 7 6 5 4 3

Contents

How to Study

The questions in this study booklet will help you discover for yourself what the Bible says. This is inductive Bible study—in which you will discover the message for yourself.

Questions are the key to inductive Bible study. Through questions you search for the writers' thoughts and ideas. The questions in this booklet are designed to help you in your quest for answers. You can and should ask your own questions too. The Bible comes alive with meaning for many people as they discover the exciting truths it contains. Our hope and prayer is that this booklet will help the Bible come alive for you.

The questions in this study are designed to be used with the New International Version of the Bible, but other translations can also be used.

Step 1. Read each Bible passage several times. Allow the ideas to sink in. Think about their meaning. Ask questions about the passage.

Step 2. Answer the questions, drawing your answers from the passage. Remember that the purpose of the study is to discover what the Bible says. Write your answers in your own words. If you use Bible study aids such as commentaries or Bible handbooks, do so only after completing your own personal study.

Step 3. Apply the Bible's message to your own life. Ask,

- What is this passage saying to me?
- How does it challenge me? Comfort me? Encourage me?
- Is there a promise I should claim? A warning I should heed?
- For what can I give thanks?

If you sense God speaking to you in some way, respond to God in a personal prayer.

Step 4. Share your thoughts with someone else if possible. This will be easiest if you are part of a Bible study group that meets regularly to share discoveries and discuss questions. If you would like to learn of a study group in your area or if you would like more information on how to start a small group Bible study,

- write to Discover Your Bible at

  2850 Kalamazoo Ave. SE   or   P.O. Box 5070
  Grand Rapids, MI 49560   STN LCD 1
                                          Burlington, ON L7R 3Y8

- call toll-free 1-888-644-0814, e-mail *smallgroups@crcna.org,* or visit *www.SmallGroupMinistries.org* (for training advice and general information)

- call toll-free 1-800-333-8300 or visit *www.FaithAliveResources.org* (to order materials)

Introduction

You are about to embark on a difficult study. Paul's writing is not easy to understand (even Peter said so). Letters that were directed to first-century Greco-Roman culture are difficult to understand today. Even if you haven't made it a practice to study your lesson before your group meets, as you study this book you may want to try to read through the material ahead of time.

But just because the material is difficult doesn't mean it's not worth studying. What you will find in these six chapters of Paul's letter could change your life. God understands the human condition, and God helped Paul to write down a message that speaks to that condition.

A little background will be helpful in your study. Picture a wide, paved road with columns along either side. This road extends from the center of the city of Ephesus to the harbor on the clear blue waters of the Mediterranean Sea. The harbor is bustling with activity. Because the city is also located on a major east-west highway, it is a center of commerce. Beyond the city lies the Coressus Mountain range, and through it runs the Cayster River. Ephesus is proud of its library, its theatre, its marketplace, and its public baths. But what sets this city apart from others like it is the temple to the Roman goddess Diana (Greek, Artemis). The Apostle Paul worked in this setting for about three years.

The choice of Ephesus as a new church plant was a wise one because of the trade route and the city's importance as the capital of the Roman province of Asia. Many people traveled through the city, and many heard Paul's message. A string of six other cities lay in a circle nearby, so letters that Paul later wrote to a church established in one city would be circulated through the rest of the churches as well.

Paul's letter was composed after he had been placed under house arrest in Rome, while awaiting trial. He lived in a house and was free to accept visitors and to correspond with people, but he was probably chained to a guard at all times. The letters to the Ephesians, the Colossians, and to Philemon were composed during this two-year period, probably sometime between A.D. 60 and 64. Unlike some of his other letters, this one was not written because of a problem in the church. Rather, Paul describes what God has in mind for the church by explaining its history. Once his readers understood God's design for the church, they would more likely be interested in the implications for their personal lives.

You too may be interested in knowing more about what God has in mind for the church and for your life. We trust this study will help you grow in your daily walk with the Lord.

Glossary of Terms

administration—carrying out a responsibility as a steward would.

apostle—one sent by God to preach the gospel. One qualification seems to be that an apostle must have seen Jesus after his resurrection. Originally the term applied to the disciples, then Paul was added, and then other missionaries. The term emphasized the authority of God, the sender.

blameless—without fault.

coming age—the time when Christ returns to judge all people and take believers to heaven.

covenants—promises that God had made with the Israelites throughout the Old Testament era. Covenants made with Abraham, Isaac, and Jacob promised that God would be with his people and that all nations of the earth would be blessed through them.

debauchery—extreme indulgence in sensuality; orgy.

Ephesus—the most important city in the Roman province of Asia (now Turkey).

evangelists—those whose primary calling is to present the gospel to the unsaved.

"Grace"—a customary Greek greeting.

heavenly realms—a phrase used frequently in Ephesians to describe all that is associated with the spiritual world, but not separate from the physical world.

holy—set apart by God to reflect God's purity.

idolator—one who sets someone or something ahead of God.

mystery—something unknown before the coming of Christ, but revealed in him. Paul uses the word twenty-one times in his writings, and six of those times are in this letter to the Ephesians.

"Peace"—a customary Hebrew greeting.

predestined—foreordained; planned or purposed by God.

prophets—those who spoke God's Word to the people. In Ephesians, this word refers to New Testament prophets.

redemption—a transaction in which one thing is given in exchange for another. Christ gave his life so that we would not have to experience eternal death as punishment for our sins.

revelation—when something that had been hidden is made known.

ruler of the kingdom of the air—Satan.

seal—something that confirms; a guarantee, assurance.

spiritual blessing—a benefit given by the Holy Spirit.

The Circumcision—a title given to Jews as a group. Because the rite of circumcision (removal of the foreskin) set Jewish males apart, this title signified the setting apart of God's chosen people.

transgressions—sins; a host of thoughts, words, and deeds "gratifying the cravings of our sinful nature and following its desires and thoughts" (Eph. 2:3).

uncircumcised—a label given by the Jews to those who were not Jewish or circumcised.

Lesson 1
Ephesians 1

God Chooses His People

1. *Ephesians 1:1-2*
   a. How does Paul describe himself? His readers?

   b. What does Paul ask God to give his readers?

2. *Ephesians 1:3-6*
   a. Why did Paul praise God?

   b. When had the Father chosen some people to be holy and blameless?

   c. What relationship do God's chosen have with God the Father and with Jesus Christ?

3. *Ephesians 1:7-10*

    a. What had Paul's readers received because of Jesus?

    b. What had God made known? When would this plan be put into effect?

    c. Under whose leadership would all things be brought together?

4. *Ephesians 1:11-14*

    a. Does God's choosing seem to be random or purposeful?

    b. Who were the first to hope in Christ?

    c. How would someone be included in God's family?

d.   What happens to those who believe?

e.   How does the Holy Spirit act as a down payment?

5.   *Ephesians 1:15-17*
   a.   Why did Paul continually give thanks for the Ephesian believers?

   b.   For what was Paul praying?

6.   *Ephesians 1:18-23*
   a.   For what enlightenment was Paul also praying?

   b.   How is God's power described?

   c.   Where is Christ now?

Questions for Reflection

a. What might the Ephesians have learned about Jesus Christ? What have you learned about Jesus from this chapter?

b. What might the Ephesians have learned about themselves? What have you learned about yourself?

c. How do you think the Ephesians felt after hearing this first part of Paul's letter? How do you feel?

Lesson 2

Ephesians 2

God Extends Grace

1. *Ephesians 2:1-3*

   In these first few verses, Paul lays out God's evaluation of the human condition.

   a.   What is the condition of those who follow the ways of this world?

   b.   Is there anyone who is exempt from this description?

2. *Ephesians 2:4-7*

   Immediately after the bleak picture he painted in the verses 1-3, Paul introduces the solution to the problem of our human condition. God "made us alive with Christ" (v. 5).

   a.   How did God feel about us?

   b.   What did God do for us? What was our condition when God did this?

c. What is our position now?

3. *Ephesians 2:8-10*

These verses talk about the place of grace in the salvation process and also about the place of good works in the life of the one who believes this message. We are saved by God's grace and through faith given by God through the Holy Spirit. The Greek word for *faith* encompasses more than intellectual assent or a decision. It means to fully rely on something or to give full assent to something. So it has to do with lifestyle as well as belief.

a. What gift did God give us?

b. What were we created to do?

4. *Ephesians 2:11-13*

Three terms must be understood in order to make sense of this portion of Ephesians 2:

The Circumcision—a title given to Jews as a group. Because the rite of circumcision set Jewish males apart, this title signified the setting apart of God's chosen people.

uncircumcised—a label given by the Jews to those who were not Jewish or circumcised.

covenants—promises that God had made with the Israelites (Jews) throughout the Old Testament era. Covenants made with Abraham, Isaac, and Jacob promised that God would be with his people and that all nations of the earth would be blessed through them.

a. What had those who were Gentiles by birth been called?

b. How would you describe their former situation?

c. What is the Gentiles' position now?

5. *Ephesians 2:14-18*
   a. How has Christ brought about peace?

   b. What was Christ's purpose?

   c. To whom do all people now have access?

6. *Ephesians 2:19-22*
   a. Describe the Gentiles' new relationship with God and with the Jews.

b.   Describe God's household (the church).

Questions for Reflection

   a.   What is the condition of each one of us apart from God?

   b.   What did God in his grace do for you?

   c.   How can you be saved?

   d.   Have you received God's grace through Christ? Do you know with certainty that you are going to heaven?

Lesson 3
Ephesians 3

God Loves His People

1. *Ephesians 3:1-3*
    a. What does Paul call himself?

    b. What does Paul assume the Ephesians already have heard?

2. *Ephesians 3:4-6*
    a. Was the mystery made known to previous generations?

    b. What is implied by the word *together?*

3. *Ephesians 3:7-9*
    a. How did Paul become a servant of the gospel?

b. How does Paul see himself? What grace was given to Paul?

4. Ephesians 3:10-13

a. What did God intend to make known to the heavenly powers? How?

b. Why are we able to approach God?

c. Why should Paul's sufferings not cause discouragement?

5. Ephesians 3:14-21

a. What did Paul want God to give to his readers?

b. What is the source of this strength?

c. Can we fully understand God's love?

d. How do verses 20-21 describe God?

Questions for Reflection
    a. What does this mystery revealed to Paul mean to you personally?

    b. What evidence do you see of the Spirit's power in your life? Do you long for Christ to be completely at home in your heart?

    c. How are you experiencing the immeasurable love of God in your life?

Lesson 4

Ephesians 4:1-24

Living Worthy Lives

1. *Ephesians 4:1-2*

   a. What kind of life were the Ephesians urged to lead?

   b. What specific instructions does Paul give?

2. *Ephesians 4:3-6*

   a. How would unity be achieved?

   b. What does each believer hold in common?

3. *Ephesians 4:7-13*

   a. What has Christ apportioned to each believer?

b. What roles (gifts) did Christ give to members of the church?

c. What was the purpose of these gifts?

4. *Ephesians 4:14-16*
   a. What kinds of dangers might an immature church face?

   b. What kind of growth did Paul expect?

   c. If the church is like a human body, how does it function for optimal growth?

5. *Ephesians 4:17-19*
   a. Describe the lives of the "Gentiles."

b. How did sin progress in their lives?

6. *Ephesians 4:20-24*

a. How had Paul's readers come to know Christ?

b. Describe what they had to put off and on.

Questions for Reflection

a. In what way are you experiencing unity in the body of Christ?

b. What spiritual gift has someone shared that has especially blessed you? What gift can you give to build up the body of Christ?

c. What have you learned about Jesus that makes you want to put on the new self?

Lesson 5
Ephesians 4:25-5:20

Good, Clean Living

1. *Ephesians 4:25-28*

    a. Why does Paul emphasize truthfulness?

    b. How could anger lead to sin?

    c. What was Paul's alternative to stealing?

2. *Ephesians 4:29-32*

    a. What kind of talk might be considered unwholesome?

    b. What might grieve the Holy Spirit?

c.   How are the sins listed in verse 31 similar?

d.   How are the qualities described in verse 32 related to what God did for us?

3.   *Ephesians 5:1-2*
   a.   How would you describe the life Paul commands?

   b.   How can we follow Christ's sacrificial giving on our behalf?

4.   *Ephesians 5:3-7*
   a.   What sins does Paul find particularly offensive? Why?

   b.   Who will be excluded from God's heavenly kingdom?

c. What causes God's wrath?

5. *Ephesians 5:8-14*

Paul calls those who accept God's gift of grace and believe in Jesus as Savior "children of light." He calls the sinful person "sleeper" and describes such people as "dead."

a. What kind of character is produced by the children of light? What is produced by darkness?

b. How does Paul want believers to react to "deeds of darkness" (sin)?

6. *Ephesians 5:15-20*

a. How should Paul's readers demonstrate wisdom?

b. What should be the most powerful influence filling their lives?

c.   What is the place of music in the life of the believer?

Questions for Reflection

a.   How does your life need to change in order to follow the guidelines Paul outlines?

b.   What opportunities are you using to live for God?

c.   Who might benefit from the "music in your heart"? Or are you in need of a song from someone else?

Lesson 6

Ephesians 5:21-6:9

Right Relationships

1. *Ephesians 5:21*

   What is the guiding principle for relationships?

2. *Ephesians 5:22-24*

   a. How are wives to relate to their husbands?

   b. What is the model for the relationship between wives and husbands?

3. *Ephesians 5:25-33*

   a. How are husbands to relate to their wives?

   b. How did Christ show his love for the church?

c. How much should a husband love his wife?

4. *Ephesians 6:1-4*
    a. How are children to relate to their parents?

    b. How are parents to relate to their children?

5. *Ephesians 6:5-9*
    a. How were slaves to relate to their masters?

    b. What was the model for the relationship between slave and master?

    c. How were masters to relate to their slaves?

d. What would motivate masters to treat their slaves well?

Questions for Reflection

a. How can Paul's advice help you in your relationships?

b. If you could do one thing to strengthen just one relationship in the next week, what would it be?

Lesson 7
Ephesians 6:10-24

Final Instructions and Greetings

1. **Ephesians 6:10-11**

    a. With what metaphor does Paul begin his final instructions?

    b. Who is commanding the opposition?

2. **Ephesians 6:12-13**

    a. Describe the enemy.

    b. What is the purpose of the armor?

3. **Ephesians 6:14-17**

    a. What pieces of armor are listed? What spiritual quality does each portray?

b. How might these spiritual qualities help people fight against the devil's schemes?

4. *Ephesians 6:18-20*
    a. How can prayer help the believer prepare for spiritual battle?

    b. For what does Paul request the prayers of the Ephesians?

5. *Ephesians 6:21-24*
    a. How is Tychicus described?

    b. What qualities does Paul include in his blessing?

Questions for Reflection
    a. How aware are you of Satan's battle in your life?

b. How do you sense God's presence, giving you the strength to stand firm?

c. What comfort do you find in Paul's final greeting?

An Invitation

Listen now to what God is saying to you.

You may be aware of things in your life that keep you from coming near to God. You may have thought of God as unsympathetic, angry, and punishing. You may feel like you don't know how to pray to God or how to come near to God.

Rejoice in the mystery of God's grace Paul reveals in Ephesians. God freely offers the "incomparable riches of his grace, expressed in his kindness to us in Christ Jesus" (Eph. 2:7), who died on the cross to save us from our sins. It doesn't matter where you come from, what you've done in the past, or what your heritage is. God has been watching over you and caring for you, drawing you closer. "And you also were included in Christ when you heard the word of truth, the gospel of your salvation" (1:13).

So now come near to God. It's as simple as A-B-C:

- **A**dmit that you have sinned and that you need God's forgiveness.
- **B**elieve that God loves you and that Jesus already paid the price for your sins.
- **C**ommit your life to God in prayer, asking God to forgive your sins, nurture you as his child, and fill you with the Holy Spirit.

Prayer of Commitment

Here is a prayer of commitment to Jesus Christ as Savior. If you long to be in a loving relationship with Jesus Christ, pray this prayer. If you have already made that commitment to Jesus, use it for renewal and praise.

Dear God, I come to you simply and honestly to confess that I have sinned, that sin is a part of who I am. And yet I know that you listen to sinners who are truthful before you. And so I come with empty hands and heart, asking for forgiveness.

I confess that only through faith in Jesus Christ can I come to you. I confess my need for a Savior, and I thank you, Jesus Christ, for dying on the cross to pay the price for my sins. I ask that you forgive my sins and count me among those who are righteous in your sight. Remove the guilt that accompanies sin and bring me to our heavenly Father.

Give me your Holy Spirit now, to help me pray and to teach me from your Word. Be my faithful God and help me to serve you faithfully. It is only because of the atoning sacrifice of Jesus Christ that I come to you, loving Father God. In Jesus' name I pray. Amen.

Evaluation Questionnaire

DISCOVER EPHESIANS

As you complete this study, please fill out this questionnaire to help us evaluate the effectiveness of our materials. Please be candid. Thank you.

1. Was this a home group ___ or a church-based ___ program? What church?

2. Was the study used for
    ___ a community evangelism group?
    ___ a community grow group?
    ___ a church Bible study group?

3. How would you rate the materials?

    Study Guide
    ___ excellent ___ very good ___ good ___ fair ___ poor

    Leader Guide
    ___ excellent ___ very good ___ good ___ fair ___ poor

4. What were the strengths?

5. What were the weaknesses?

6. What would you suggest to improve the material?

7. In general, what was the experience of your group?

Your name (optional) _____

Address _____

8. Other comments:

(Please fold, tape, stamp, and mail. Thank you.)

Faith Alive Christian Resources
2850 Kalamazoo Ave. SE
Grand Rapids, MI 49560